ABOUT HABITATS

Oceans

To the One who created oceans.

—*Genesis* 1:9–10

Published by
PEACHTREE PUBLISHERS
1700 Chattahoochee Avenue
Atlanta, Georgia 30318-2112
www.peachtree-online.com

Illustrations created in watercolor on archival quality 100% rag watercolor paper.
Text and titles set in Novarese from Adobe.

Printed in September 2011 by Imago in Singapore
10 9 8 7 6 5 4 3 2 1
First Edition

Library of Congress Cataloging-in-Publication Data

Sill, Cathryn P., 1953-
  About habitats : oceans / Cathryn Sill ; illustrated by John Sill.
    p. cm.
  ISBN 978-1-56145-618-5 / 1-56145-618-7
  1. Ocean--Juvenile literature. 2. Marine ecology--Juvenile literature. I. Sill, John, ill.
II. Title.
  GC21.5.S55 2012
  578.77--dc23
                        2011020466

Oceans

Written by **Cathryn Sill** Illustrated by **John Sill**

PEACHTREE
ATLANTA

OCEANS FEATURED IN THIS BOOK

PLEASE NOTE: Map and ocean areas are not to scale.

Oceans

Oceans are huge bodies of salt water that cover most of Earth.

All the world's oceans are joined together.

PLATE 2
PLANET EARTH

The bottom of the ocean is often called the ocean floor. Parts of it are flat.

Other places on the ocean floor have the world's tallest mountains and deepest valleys.

Ocean water is always moving.

The water in oceans may be warm
and tropical…

...or cold and frozen.

PLATE 7
ARCTIC OCEAN

Beluga Whale

Plants that live in oceans need sunshine to grow.

They live in shallow water or float near the top where there is more light.

Most ocean animals live near the top of
the water where there is plenty of sunlight.

Some live in the dim light between the surface and the bottom of the ocean.

Fewer animals live in the deepest parts of oceans where it is cold and dark.

Animals that live in oceans move in different ways.

a.

b.

c.

d.

e.

Some always stay in one place.

PLATE 13
PACIFIC AND INDIAN
OCEANS

Giant Clam

Many ocean animals eat meat.

PLATE 14
ATLANTIC OCEAN

Atlantic Sailfish
(also shown: Sardines)

Others eat plants.

PLATE 15
TROPICAL AND
SUBTROPICAL OCEANS
WORLDWIDE

Green Sea Turtle

Ocean animals need ways to stay safe.
They may hide, swim together in schools,
attack enemies, or use poison.

a.

b.

c.

d.

Oceans provide food, jobs, transportation, and recreation for people all over the world. They are important places that need to be protected.

Afterword

PLATE 1

Oceans cover 71 percent of Earth. All ocean water is salty. Most of the salt comes from land. The salt found in soil and rocks is dissolved in water and washed into the oceans by rivers. Underwater volcanoes also add salt to the ocean. Albatrosses spend most of their lives gliding over the ocean looking for food such as fish and squid. Wandering Albatrosses have the largest wingspan (up to 11 $\frac{1}{2}$ feet or 3.5 m) of any bird in the world. They live in the Southern Ocean.

PLATE 2

There are five oceans in the world. The Pacific, Atlantic, Indian, Southern, and Arctic Oceans are all connected to form one World Ocean. Smaller bodies of water linked to oceans are called seas and gulfs. Earth is sometimes called the Blue Planet because the huge size of the ocean causes it to look blue from outer space.

PLATE 3

The area of the ocean floor around the edge of each continent is called the continental shelf. It slopes out gently for many miles. Much of the deep ocean floor is covered by flat places called abyssal plains. Some rays live along the bottom of the ocean on the continental shelf. Their flat bodies help them hide and hunt. Southern Stingrays use the venomous spine on their tails to defend themselves. They live in the western Atlantic Ocean, Gulf of Mexico, and Caribbean Sea.

PLATE 4

Mountains beneath the ocean are called seamounts. Many seamounts are under thousands of feet of water. The tops of some of these mountains rise above the ocean's surface to form islands. The deep valleys on the ocean floor are called trenches. Scalloped Hammerheads (a type of shark) sometimes swim in large schools around seamounts. They live in temperate and tropical waters all over the world.

PLATE 5

Waves, tides, and currents keep ocean water in constant motion. Wind blowing across the surface of the ocean creates waves. Tides cause the ocean level to rise and fall two times a day in most places. Currents are streams of water that move continuously in a certain direction throughout oceans. Short-beaked Common Dolphins are marine mammals that live in warm temperate and tropical waters of the Pacific and Atlantic Oceans.

PLATE 6

Oceans closest to Earth's equator are tropical. Coral reefs are found in the warm waters of tropical oceans. Some anemones and clownfish live together on coral reefs. Anemones catch food by grabbing and stinging small animals with their tentacles. Clownfish are covered with slimy mucus that protects them from the stings. Clownfish stay safe from enemies by living among the anemones' tentacles. They help the anemones by eating tiny animals and plants that cause them harm.

PLATE 7

The coldest ocean waters are near the North and South Poles. In winter the surfaces of polar oceans freeze over. Many animals are able to live below the ice. Animals that need to breathe air must stay near breathing holes. Beluga Whales live in the chilly Arctic Ocean. They are sometimes called sea canaries because of the whistling sounds they make.

PLATE 8

Giant Kelp is the largest ocean plant and one of the fastest growing plants in the world. It can grow up to 24 inches (60 cm) a day. Giant Kelp makes dense forests in shallow water in the northeast Pacific and in temperate waters of southern oceans. Sargassum Seaweed drifts in large mats on the surface in parts of the ocean. Many animals such as the Sargassumfish live in Sargassum Seaweed. Sargassumfish inhabit tropical and subtropical oceans around the world.

PLATE 9

The top layer of the ocean is called the sunlit zone. Tiny plants and animals called plankton are plentiful in the sunlit zone. Plankton provides food for many ocean animals, including flyingfish. Larger animals often feed on those that eat plankton. Flyingfish are able to escape from predators by jumping out of the water and gliding through the air. Blackwing Flyingfish live in subtropical oceans around the world.

PLATE 10

The middle zone of the ocean is called the twilight zone. It has little sunlight. Sperm Whales come to the surface to breathe, but they dive to the twilight zone to hunt for squid. They are able to stay underwater for up to two hours. Sperm Whales live in deep waters in all the oceans. Giant Squid can be up to 59 feet (18m) long. They are rarely seen in the wild. Their remains have been found in the stomachs of Sperm Whales. Giant Squid probably live in all the oceans.

PLATE 11

The deep part of the ocean that gets no sunlight is called the midnight zone. There is little food in this region. Some animals that live there eat dead plants and animals that have drifted down from the surface. Other deep ocean dwellers have long sharp teeth for catching prey. Humpback Anglerfish have glowing lures that cause curious animals to come close to their large mouths. Anglerfish live in all the oceans.

PLATE 12

Portuguese Men-of-War use their gas-filled balloons to float on the surface of the warm oceans around the world. Giant Octopuses swim in the Pacific Ocean by drawing water into their bodies and forcing it out in a powerful squirt. Striped Remoras hitch rides. They have suction cups on the top of their heads, which they use to attach themselves to animals such as Blacktip Reef Sharks. Remoras live in all warm oceans. Fiordland Penguins dive and swim in the Pacific Ocean. Spiny Lobsters walk along the ocean floor in the Western Atlantic Ocean, Gulf of Mexico, and Caribbean Sea.

PLATE 13

Animals that stay in one place without moving are called sessile. Giant Clams fasten themselves on coral reefs and sit there for the rest of their lives. Their bright colors come from algae that live in the clams and provide them with food. These clams also feed by filtering plankton from the water. They can be over 4 feet (120 cm) long and weigh over 500 pounds (225 kg). Giant Clams live in the Indian and South Pacific Oceans.

PLATE 14

Animals that eat meat are called carnivores. Large carnivores usually eat smaller animals. The smaller animals eat animals and plants that are even smaller. This is called a food chain. Adult Atlantic Sailfish have no predators and are at the top of their food chain. They eat small fish such as sardines. Sardines eat the tiny marine animals and plants called plankton. Atlantic Sailfish live in the Atlantic Ocean and Mediterranean Sea.

PLATE 15

Animals that eat plants are called herbivores. Adult Green Sea Turtles eat ocean plants such as seagrasses and algae. Green Sea Turtles are endangered because people hunt and eat them and their eggs, and because land development destroys their nesting sites. Pollution sometimes ruins the seagrass beds that provide food for them. Green Sea Turtles live in tropical and subtropical oceans around the world.

PLATE 16

Leafy Sea Dragons look almost exactly like some types of seaweed. These fish can easily hide from enemies in seaweed beds. They live in the Indian Ocean along the southern coast of Australia. Yellow and Bluebacked Fusiliers often form large schools that can confuse predators. They inhabit parts of the tropical Indian and Pacific Oceans. Blue Crabs, which live in the western Atlantic Ocean, snap their claws aggressively when threatened. Red Lionfish defend themselves with venomous spines located on their fins. They are native to the Indian and Pacific Oceans but have been introduced to other places.

PLATE 17

All of the oceans together provide the largest habitat and support the greatest variety of life on Earth. Oceans influence the world's climate. They provide many natural resources such as oil, salt, and other valuable minerals. Oceans are an important source of oxygen. In spite of their huge size, oceans have been harmed by human activity. Pollution and overfishing are two major threats to the well-being of oceans. Healthy oceans are necessary for healthy people.

GLOSSARY

BIOME—an area such as a grassland or wetland that shares the same types of plants and animals
ECOSYSTEM—a community of living things and their environment
HABITAT—the place where animals and plants live

Camouflage—colors or patterns on an animal that help it hide
Continent—one of seven main masses of land on the earth
Equator—an imaginary line around the center of the earth halfway between the North and South Poles
Predator—an animal that lives by hunting and eating other animals
Prey—an animal that is hunted and eaten by a predator
School—a large group of one kind of fish
Subtropical—next to the tropics
Temperate—not very hot and not very cold
Tropical—the area near the equator that is hot year-round
Venom—poison injected by an animal

BIBLIOGRAPHY

BOOKS

EYE WONDER: OCEAN by Samantha Gray (DK Publishing, Inc.)
OCEANS AND SEAS by Nicola Davies (Kingfisher Publications)
THE BLUE PLANET SEAS OF LIFE: OCEAN WORLD by David Orme and Helen Bird (BBC Worldwide Limited, Scholastic Inc.)
THE MAGIC SCHOOLBUS ON THE OCEAN FLOOR by Joanna Cole and Bruce Degen (Scholastic Inc.)

WEBSITES

http://www.globio.org/glossopedia/article.aspx?art_id=69&art_nm=Oceans
http://www.wwf.panda.org/about_our_earth/ecoregions/about/habitat_types/habitats/oceans/
http://ocean.nationalgeographic.com/ocean/?source=NavEnvOcean
http://www.mbgnet.net/

ISBN 978-1-56145-234-7 HC
ISBN 978-1-56145-312-2 PB

ISBN 978-1-56145-038-1 HC
ISBN 978-1-56145-364-1 PB

ISBN 978-1-56145-028-2 HC
ISBN 978-1-56145-147-0 PB

ISBN 978-1-56145-301-6 HC
ISBN 978-1-56145-405-1 PB

ISBN 978-1-56145-256-9 HC
ISBN 978-1-56145-335-1 PB

ISBN 978-1-56145-588-1 HC

ISBN 978-1-56145-207-1 HC
ISBN 978-1-56145-232-3 PB

ISBN 978-1-56145-141-8 HC
ISBN 978-1-56145-174-6 PB

ISBN 978-1-56145-358-0 HC
ISBN 978-1-56145-407-5 PB

ISBN 978-1-56145-331-3 HC
ISBN 978-1-56145-406-8 PB

ISBN 978-1-56145-488-4 HC

ISBN 978-1-56145-454-9 HC

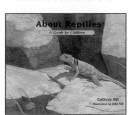

ISBN 978-1-56145-183-8 HC
ISBN 978-1-56145-233-0 PB

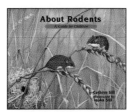

ISBN 978-1-56145-454-9 HC

ABOUT HABITATS SERIES

Deserts

ISBN 978-1-56145-390-0 HC

Grasslands

ISBN 978-1-56145-559-1 HC

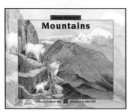

Mountains

ISBN 978-1-56145-469-3 HC

Wetlands

ISBN 978-1-56145-432-7 HC

Oceans

ISBN 978-1-56145-618-5 HC

THE SILLS

Cathryn Sill, a former elementary school teacher, is the author of the acclaimed ABOUT… series. With her husband John and her brother-in-law Ben Sill, she coauthored the popular bird-guide parodies, A FIELD GUIDE TO LITTLE-KNOWN AND SELDOM-SEEN BIRDS OF NORTH AMERICA, ANOTHER FIELD GUIDE TO LITTLE-KNOWN AND SELDOM-SEEN BIRDS OF NORTH AMERICA, and BEYOND BIRDWATCHING.

John Sill is a prize-winning and widely published wildlife artist who illustrated the ABOUT… series and illustrated and coauthored the FIELD GUIDES and BEYOND BIRDWATCHING. A native of North Carolina, he holds a B.S. in Wildlife Biology from North Carolina State University.

The Sills live in Franklin, North Carolina.